A Is for Abinadi

Praise for *A Is for Abinadi*

"*A Is for Abinadi* is a delightful book for children to learn about the great men and women in our scriptures. As a mom and grandma, I so appreciate any book that will help reinforce the scriptures and making faithful choices. I loved the illustrations and the silly parts as well. This book is perfect for engaging young children and teaching and entertaining at the same time! Kudos to Heidi and Jason on a terrific book!"
—Merrilee Boyack, author, speaker, life coach, and community leader

"I can't praise *A Is for Abinadi* enough! Children will love the adorable illustrations that complement these short and delightful summations of scripture heroes. And adults will appreciate the great reminder of who's who in the scriptures. A fun and charming book to share over and over with the children in your life."
—H.B. Moore, author of Best of State &
Whitney Award-winning novel, *Abinadi*

"Poelman and Pruett have created an entertaining and engaging ABC book guaranteed to excite readers of all ages. Using the standard works as their foundation, they build the framework for children to delve and dig into the scriptures themselves."
—Annalisa Hall, author of *The Holy Ghost Is like a Blanket*

A Is for Abinadi

An Alphabet Book of Scripture Heroes

Written by Heidi Poelman

Illustrated by Jason Pruett

CFI
An Imprint of Cedar Fort, Inc.
Springville, Utah

ISBN 13: 978-1-4621-1369-9

Published by CFI, an imprint of Cedar Fort, Inc.
2373 W. 700 S., Springville, UT 84663
Distributed by Cedar Fort, Inc., www.cedarfort.com

LIBRARY OF CONGRESS CATALOGING-IN-PUBLICATION DATA

Poelman, Heidi N., 1980- author.
A is for Abinadi : an alphabet book of scripture heroes / written by Heidi N. Poelman ; illustrated by Jason Pruett.
pages cm
ISBN 978-1-4621-1369-9 (alk. paper)
1. Book of Mormon--Biography--Juvenile literature. 2. English language--Alphabet--Juvenile literature.
3. Alphabet books. [1. Alphabet.] I. Pruett, Jason, 1980- illustrator. II. Title.

BX8627.3.P64 2013
289.3'22--dc23

2013033030.

Cover and interior layout design by Shawnda T. Craig
Cover design © 2013 Lyle Mortimer
Edited by Catherine Christensen and Emily S. Chambers

Printed in the United States of America

10 9 8 7 6 5 4 3

For Scott, Zach, Ellie, and Addie.
—Heidi

For Aspen, Hannah, Lincoln, and Ian.
—Jason

IS FOR ABINADI. Heavenly Father asked Abinadi to preach repentance to the wicked King Noah and his priests. Abinadi was killed for following God, but because of his bravery, the priest Alma listened and became a great prophet.

B

IS FOR THE BROTHER OF JARED.
The brother of Jared needed a way to light his people's ships. He gathered 16 stones and asked for the Lord's help. Because of the brother of Jared's great faith, the Lord made the stones glow.

C IS FOR CAPTAIN MORONI. Captain Moroni used the title of liberty to help his people stand up against the Lamanites. He reminded his armies that they were fighting for their homes, their families, and their freedom.

IN MEMORY OF OUR GOD, OUR RELIGION, AND FREEDOM, AND OUR PEACE, OUR WIVES, AND OUR CHILDREN

D IS FOR DANIEL. Daniel chose to pray, even when that meant breaking the law. Wicked men threw Daniel in a lion's den. Because of Daniel's faith, Heavenly Father protected him.

E IS FOR EVE. Eve lived with Adam in the Garden of Eden. She made the decision to eat the forbidden fruit so she could learn about right and wrong, joy and pain. Because of her decision, Adam and Eve were able to have children and begin Heavenly Father's great plan of happiness.

F IS FOR FATHER ABRAHAM. God asked Father Abraham to sacrifice his only child. Abraham was willing to do anything God asked. Abraham proved his obedience and was allowed to keep his son. God then blessed Abraham with many children.

IS FOR GIDEON. Gideon was a wise Nephite captain. He helped King Limhi make tough decisions in times of battle. When the Nephites were held captive by the Lamanites, Gideon created a plan to help the Nephite people escape.

IS FOR HANNAH. Hannah wanted to have a child more than anything. One day, she made a promise to the Lord. Hannah promised that if she could have a child, she would let him live a life of service in the temple. Hannah kept her promise. Her son, Samuel, became a great prophet.

I IS FOR ISAIAH. Isaiah was a wise prophet who lived long before Jesus was born. He had a vision of Jesus coming to earth as a newborn baby. He wrote down the prophecy so others could await the birth of their Savior.

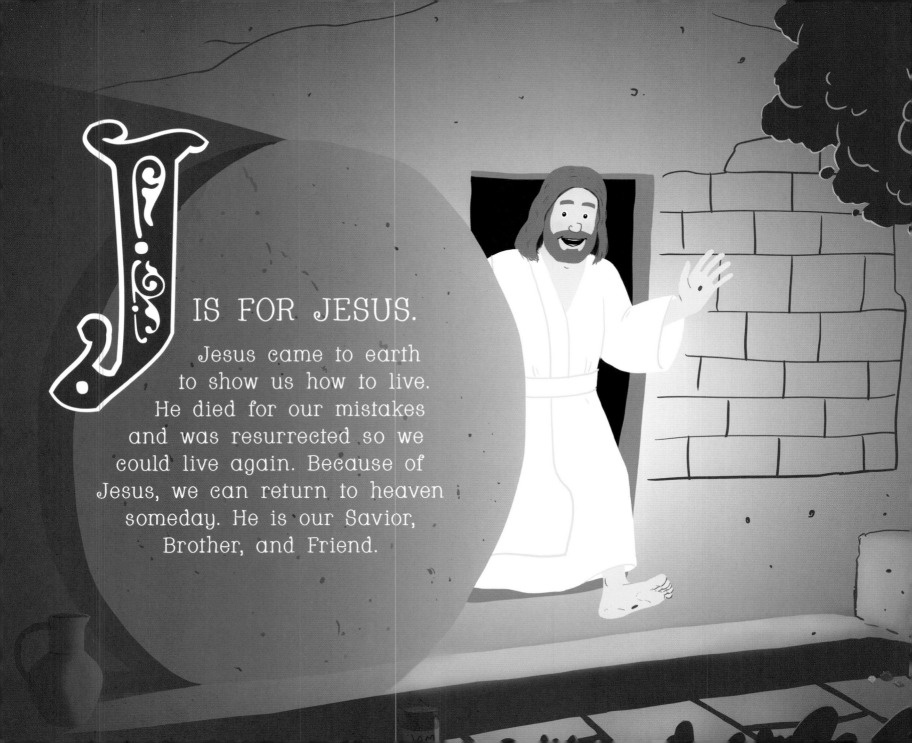

J

IS FOR JESUS.

Jesus came to earth to show us how to live. He died for our mistakes and was resurrected so we could live again. Because of Jesus, we can return to heaven someday. He is our Savior, Brother, and Friend.

K IS FOR KING BENJAMIN.
King Benjamin was a righteous leader.
He stood on a tower and taught his people
about loving God and serving each other.

L IS FOR LEHI. Lehi was a prophet who warned his people to repent. He said that if they did not listen, their city would be destroyed. Many people laughed at him, but Lehi knew what he said was true. He led his family away to keep them safe.

IS FOR MARY. Mary was a special young woman. Heavenly Father chose her to be the mother of Jesus. She gave birth to the Savior in a humble stable. She helped her Son prepare for His ministry on earth.

N IS FOR NEPHI. Nephi always chose to obey Heavenly Father, no matter how hard the task. He saved the brass plates from wicked Laban. When God asked Nephi to build a ship, he didn't complain. Nephi was a righteous example to his brothers.

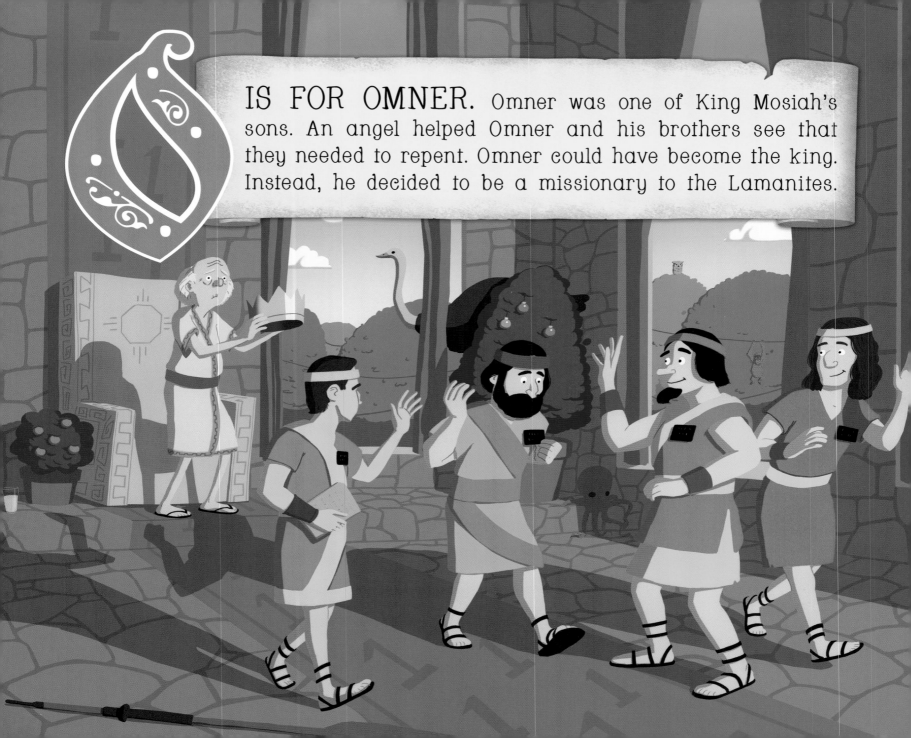

IS FOR OMNER. Omner was one of King Mosiah's sons. An angel helped Omner and his brothers see that they needed to repent. Omner could have become the king. Instead, he decided to be a missionary to the Lamanites.

P IS FOR PETER. Peter was one of the Twelve Apostles. One day, Peter was in his boat when he saw Jesus coming toward him on the water. Jesus called for Peter to come. Peter had such faith that he jumped out of his boat. For a moment he walked on the water to meet the Savior.

IS FOR QUEEN ESTHER.
Queen Esther knew that her people were about to be harmed by order of the king. Queen Esther stood up for the Jews. She bravely convinced the king to keep them safe.

R IS FOR REBEKAH. One day, a man went looking for a caring woman who could marry his master, Isaac. He came to a well and asked for a drink. Rebekah got a drink for him, and then she helped his camels get water too. Because of her kindness, the man knew she was the right woman.

S IS FOR SAMUEL THE LAMANITE.

Heavenly Father asked Samuel the Lamanite to teach repentance. When the people locked him out, Samuel preached on the city wall. When the people shot arrows and threw stones, Samuel stood firm. Heavenly Father protected him.

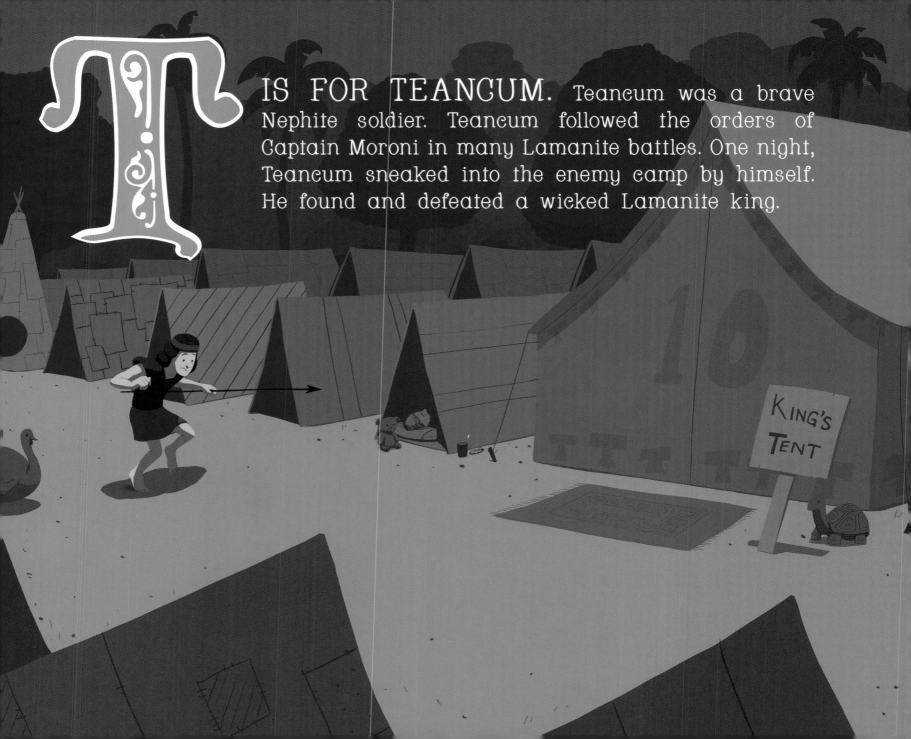

T IS FOR TEANCUM. Teancum was a brave Nephite soldier. Teancum followed the orders of Captain Moroni in many Lamanite battles. One night, Teancum sneaked into the enemy camp by himself. He found and defeated a wicked Lamanite king.

KING'S TENT

U

IS FOR URIAH THE HITTITE.

Uriah the Hittite was one of King David's most valiant soldiers. Uriah left everything he had to go to the front lines of battle to fight for his king.

V IS FOR VISITING ANGEL.

The angel Moroni came to visit Joseph Smith many times to teach him about the gold plates. Hundreds of years before, Moroni buried the gold plates in the midst of battle to keep them safe. The angel Moroni helped Joseph find them so we could read them today.

W

IS FOR WISE MEN. The wise men waited many years for a sign marking the birth of Jesus. On the night the star appeared, the wise men knew Jesus had come. They packed their bags along with gifts of gold, frankincense, and myrrh. Then they left to find the newborn King.

X IS FOR EXODUS OF THE ISRAELITES.

The exodus was a great journey. The Israelites left a life of slavery in search of freedom. The Israelites followed the prophet Moses in the wilderness for 40 years.

Y IS FOR YOUNG WARRIORS. The stripling warriors were 2,000 young soldiers who followed Helaman into battle. Their mothers taught them to believe in Heavenly Father and Jesus. Because of their faith, not one soldier was killed.

Z IS FOR ZORAM. Zoram helped Nephi get the brass plates from the wicked Laban. Zoram always kept his promises and was a true friend to Nephi.

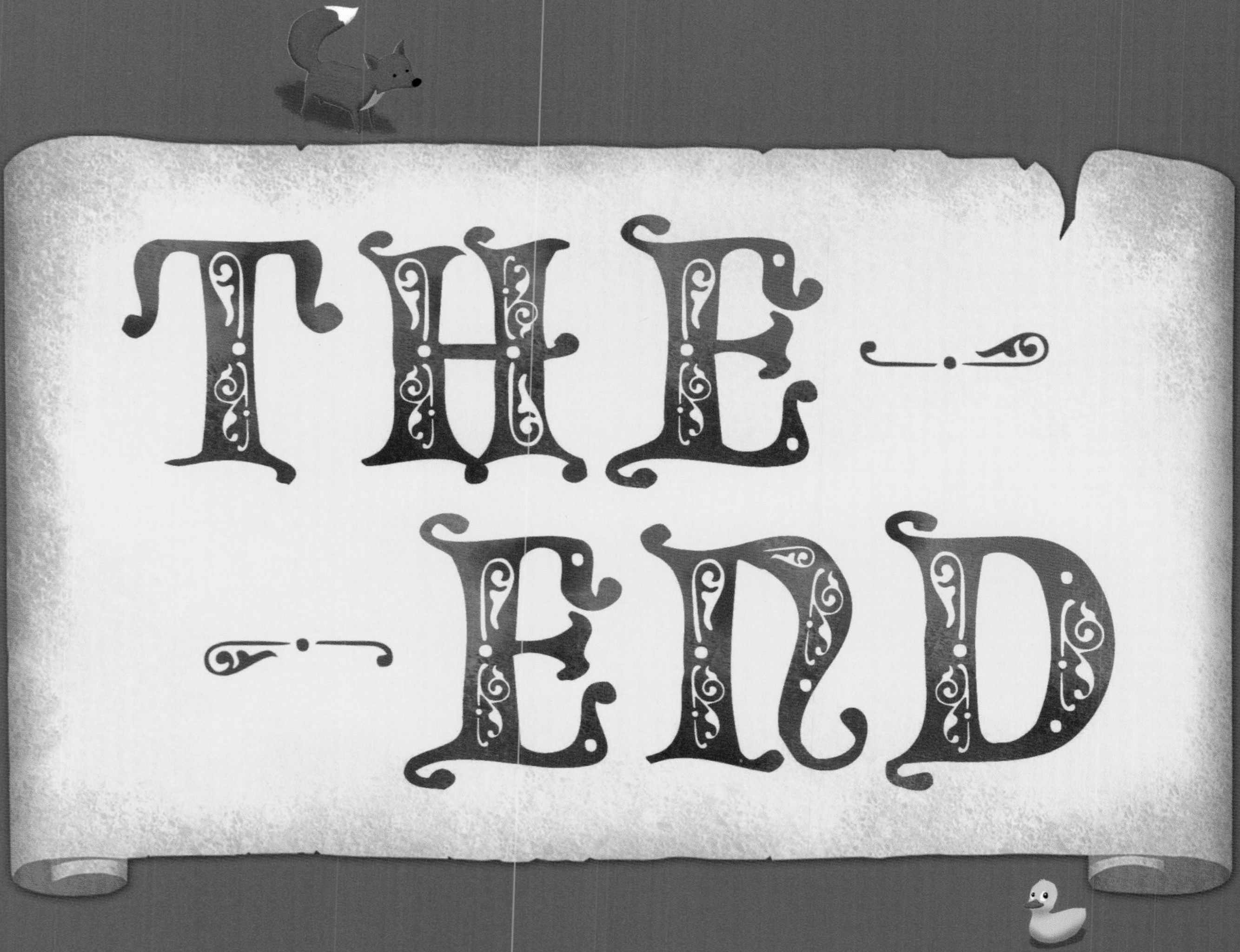
THE END

About the Author

Heidi Poelman

has always loved learning about inspiring people. In *A is for Abinadi*, she found a way to write about many of her favorites. Heidi received her degrees in communication from Brigham Young University (BA) and Wake Forest University (MA). She lives in Utah with her husband and three children.

About the Illustrator

JASON PRUETT

has always loved making people smile. Jason has degrees in art from Brigham Young University (BFA) and the Academy of Art University (MFA). He lives in Los Angeles with his wife where he creates drawings that make people smile.